LIFE AFTER Lupus

"The Healing Process"

Luther T. Collins

LIFE AFTER Lupus "The Healing Process"
Luther T. Collins

Printed in the United States of America

Published by: Legacy Voice Productions

Copyright © 2025 by Luther T. Collins

All rights reserved. This book or parts thereof may not be reproduced in any form, stored in a retrieval system, or transmitted in any form by any means-electronic, mechanical, photocopy, recording, or otherwise-without prior written permission of the author, except as provided by United States of America copyright law.

ISBN: 978-1-960179-38-8

To contact author for booking or ordering additional copies, go to: legacyvoiceproductions@gmail.com

LIFE AFTER Lupus "The Healing Process"
Luther T. Collins

Table of Contents

Segment 1 – The Sickness

Segment 2 – Denial

Segment 3 – The Road to Recovery

Segment 4 – Back to Business

Segment 5 – Testing the Limits

Segment 6 – Moving Forward

Segment 7 – Life After

Segment 8 – Letter & Poem
                     Thank you MCV

LIFE AFTER Lupus "The Healing Process"
Luther T. Collins

Segment 1 – The Sickness

February 24, 2013, was the day that my life changed forever. The previous six weeks leading up till this date I experienced constant fevers, dry coughs, scaly alopecia, painful fingertips, fatigue, painful rashes all over, and body chills. What started as somewhat a normal day became far from it as the day evolved. I will never forget this day as long as I live.

During this time, I was a store manager at Finish Line in Richmond, VA. I began my journey with Finish Line in February of 2011 as an Assistant Manager and was determined to work my way up. I had just completed MIT training and was promoted to GM of the store in September of 2012. Our store went from past poor performances to doing well in a short period of time. We had an amazing staff as we were

LIFE AFTER Lupus "The Healing Process"
Luther T. Collins

getting companywide attention because of our sudden success.

Our store would go from a 1.3-million-dollar store to a 1.7-million-dollar store as we were trending 2 million during my time in charge. We were in the rebuilding and recreating stage of our store during this time. My biggest asset was my team as I ensured my managers and top associates knew everything, I knew including how to run the store in my absence. Not knowing that this would be the case, everything in question would be tested.

On the night that everything changed for me I would become sick at work outside of the norm. I had constant chills, was running a fever, sweating heavily, coughing, losing my color, and the list goes on. Two of my top associates were closing with me that evening. It got so bad that I just went and sat down on a bench in the front of the store as one of my workers called

LIFE AFTER Lupus "The Healing Process"
Luther T. Collins

my wife. She, not knowing the seriousness, probably saved my life. Even though I was weak and hurt I tried to downplay it as I hung in there for a couple of hours until we closed at 9pm.

When my wife came and got me from work, she said I was blue. After seeing that I didn't look well she decided to take me to one of the top hospitals in VA, VCU. I got to the emergency room, and they immediately went to work on me. I remember being told we don't know what's wrong with you, Mr. Collins, but you're not leaving until we figure it out. My wife never said it to me, but I know this alone gave her major relief knowing that something clearly was wrong with me.

Prior to going to the emergency room on this day I went to 3 other emergency rooms within the last 6 weeks and was misdiagnosed. I was told I had bronchitis, hemoptysis, and fevers. I was treated and given medication like

LIFE AFTER Lupus "The Healing Process"
Luther T. Collins

Zithromax, ibuprofen, etc. and sent home immediately after each visit. Not knowing what was going on was concerning, especially considering I was healthy and never had any serious health issues in my life.

I was immediately admitted into the hospital as this by far was the quickest ER visit that I have ever experienced. My paperwork revealed I was fatigued and ill, appearing upon arrival. When admitted I had an erythematous rash on my arms, chest, and back. In addition to this I had bluish discoloration on my fingers as well as around my mouth. I also had photosensitivity, a fever that exceeded 104, chills, and a nasty cough.

My initial labs that were taken revealed a pancytopenia and abdominal/pelvis CT showing multiple mildly enlarged lymph nodes and splenomegaly. They immediately gave me a high dose of prednisone and pain medication to break the fever. My first 3 days in the

LIFE AFTER Lupus "The Healing Process"
Luther T. Collins

hospital I ran a constant fever above 102. I remember seeing 4 and 5 doctors at one time at least 3 times a day.

I would wake up in the middle of the night consistently pouring down sweat having to change my hospital gown at least two to three times a night. The chills as well as the hurtful cough just would not go away. Although I wasn't prepared for death I wasn't sure I would make it out of this alive. It was very challenging both mentally and physically being in this position. I was so used to being the provider, the protector, the comforter, the counselor, and the motivator.

I believed in God and trusted God at this point in my life. However, my faith for myself was shaky at best. I always believed God could do it for everyone else. But I always doubted and questioned, would God do it for me? I guess with all the bad decisions and choices I made in life at this stage I just

LIFE AFTER Lupus "The Healing Process"
Luther T. Collins

felt like it may be karma catching up with me.

At the time I was working full time as a store manager at Finish Line, just recently resigned as a part time server at Ihop, and currently enrolled at Strayer University working towards my bachelor's in business. I enjoyed helping people, meeting people, and providing a light in dark places.

In my personal life my wife and I had just gotten back together good after a brief separation. My wife moved out taking our baby girl who would have been two years old at the time and my stepdaughter who I was struggling to have a productive relationship with at the time. Four years into our marriage and finally, just beginning to gain momentum with a do over.

Through it all my wife, my family, my Pastor, my church family, my coworkers, the hospital staff, and the

LIFE AFTER Lupus "The Healing Process"
Luther T. Collins

doctors remained by my side faithfully. At this stage I am curious to know how many honestly were confident I would truly make it. There was no shortage of flowers, cards, phone calls, and constant visits. The overwhelming amount of love, support, and prayers are what kept me alive and fighting. This would be outside of Gods mercy, grace, and plan for my life that I had no clue about of course.

My wife never left my side as she made sure everyone knew that I was in the hospital and how serious it was. My wife was the love of my life and I drew strength from her dedication and devotion to stay by my side. I remember her being there in the middle of the night to change me frequently as if I was a baby. I remember her calling on the doctors when I was in pain and needed help. I remember her helping me get out of bed at all hours just to use the bathroom or shower. She was always on me about eating and keeping my

LIFE AFTER Lupus "The Healing Process"
Luther T. Collins

strength up. She was my biggest supporter and the one who believed in me even when I didn't believe in myself.

Tasha I will always be indebted to you for the love, strength, devotion, dedication, and fight you displayed during one of the toughest battles in my life. I can also hear you saying, you are not going to make me a widow leaving me with two babies especially when you do not have any life insurance for us, lol. I thank God for you staying by my side when you could have easily walked away or throwed in the towel.

I remember my mother visiting me frequently as she even brought Jailyn and Man, my kids from my first marriage. I never heard them say it but I truly believe that they may have been in fear as I was always a workaholic, inherited honestly but I always came through for my family starting at a young age. And to see me like this is probably something they could have

LIFE AFTER Lupus "The Healing Process"
Luther T. Collins

never envisioned. My mom would bring plenty of family to see me during this time frame. She always brought my aunt's, cousins, and family members who could not drive as well as just keeping everyone in the loop on my status.

Some of my aunts came to see me during this time. My Aunt Brenda was probably the closest to me at the time as she was the one person I could talk to about anything. She would later pass away from cancer not too long afterwards but she had to be there as she always represented strength to me.

She wore a hat as this was never her style, not the pretty lady with long black curly hair. I later heard that she was losing her hair at that time and was wearing wigs. She always came in smiling leaving me with lots of love and encouragement as she never left my side. She stayed around long enough to make sure I was good to keep the legacy and namesake alive is how I see it. My other aunts were all amazing as they were present. I remember seeing Aunt Joyce, Aunt Vonnie, Aunt Dot, Aunt Margaret, Aunt Kathy, and even some whom I did not know their names.

My cousins came in flocks as my family is big. My mom has six sisters and three brothers just to give you an idea. This doesn't include my wife's family who would also be present. My dad's side is big too, but I don't know much of them and he was incarcerated at the time I was fighting for my life. My dad and I never consistently had a productive relationship ever.

One cousin in particular who always came with my mom is Jewel. I call her my aunt/cousin as she's closer in age to my mom and she along with her amazing mom, Aunt Virginia who went home to be with the Lord some time ago. Her mom and my grandma, Margaret Valentine whom I never got to

LIFE AFTER Lupus "The Healing Process"
Luther T. Collins

meet were sisters. Aunt Jewel had just been released from the hospital not too long before me. She knew what it was like to fight for your life as she had a brain tumor and a lot of people had given up on her and even walked away from her.

I remember visiting her in the hospital just before it was my time to go in. She could not talk and was not always aware but I'm sure she could hear me. Jewel had always been one of my favorites as she and I had history that goes far beyond the surface and was there for me for many tough moments in my life. She is strong, she is a survivor, and she is a walking, talking, and breathing miracle. Her smile was her strength which would now become my strength.

My Pastor at the time, Apostle Vanessa Thomas came and visited me. She was not alone as she always traveled with the late, great Elder James. I remember my

LIFE AFTER Lupus "The Healing Process"
Luther T. Collins

Pastor telling me God was going to heal me. She also said you're going to write a book about your testimony and how God healed you. I remember her and Elder James praying for me and telling me to hang in there. They not only believed in me, but they encouraged me to keep fighting, keep believing, and most importantly keep praying.

The overall support would be overwhelming, but it was what I needed. My family on my side as well as my wife's side were all present and calling constantly for updates. My work family did the same as they called pretty frequently to check in on me. There was no shortage of gifts, balloons, flowers, cards, phone calls, and visits during this time. My room looked like a gift shop as it was the love and support that gave me life when I thought I was dying.

To be honest I don't remember how long I was in the hospital. I believe it was much greater than a week but shorter than a month. I can't recall exactly; I just remember it felt like an eternity. The pain was unbearable at times as it constantly felt like my skin was enflamed. This of course was in addition to the many other symptoms I was experiencing at the time. God knew who to send to my bedside for prayers, encouragement, and to speak life to what appeared a dead situation.

I was officially diagnosed with lupus of the skin also known as cutaneous. This is a chronic autoimmune skin disease that causes sores and rashes all over the skin. The sun was not my friend, and my body was under attack. My skin was scaly as I had red and thick rashes and sores all over my body. These sores and rashes would itch and burn causing maximum discomfort.

While in the hospital I was hooked-up to every machine you could imagine. I had to have a skin biopsy done in multiple areas of my body including my

LIFE AFTER Lupus "The Healing Process"
Luther T. Collins

scalp. Yes, they stuck a needle in my head to remove some of my skin, most definitely not fun. I had to have so much blood drawn every hour on the hour everyday for numerous tests. I was hardly able to sleep as the pain, discomfort, irritation, agony, soreness, affliction, and torment appeared to be unbearable.

From the time I was hospitalized and diagnosed with lupus until I was released, I can truly say it was nothing but God that kept me. There is no other explanation I could possibly give. When I should have died sitting on the bench at work, on the way to the hospital, and in that hospital bed, God said not so. The only reason I'm here today to tell my story is because of his grace and his mercy. I thank God for the skilled doctors, amazing nurses, entire VCU Staff, family, friends, coworkers, Pastors, Elders, Ministers, church family, etc. Even with all the love and support, all I can say is God did that!

Chapter 2 – Denial

After what appeared to be a long hospital stay mentally and physically, I was released from VCU. I've always considered myself to have an S on my chest, so it was easy for me to allow denial to set in. First, I really had no clue what lupus was and had never heard of it before being diagnosed. Nobody in my family or nobody I knew of personally had lupus so this was something I could not comprehend. This was beyond me as the only comparison I could make was the similarities to cancer.

I was sent home with several medications as this was all so new to me considering I had never been one to take any medications at any point in my life. Prednisone was my least favorite of the medications that I was prescribed. Not only did I have an extremely high dosage of prednisone, but it would soon

LIFE AFTER Lupus "The Healing Process"
Luther T. Collins

begin packing on the pounds. While I easily lost 15 to 20 pounds in the hospital, I was not mentally prepared for the 50 plus pounds that I would easily put on. Not only did my appetite increase but I was very limited in what I could do. If I remember correctly, I had to stay home 2 to 3 weeks before I was released to return to work.

I was in so much denial that shortly after being released from the hospital I attempted to wing myself off the medication. I would do this multiple times as I was determined to get rid of this disease. In doing so I eventually winded up back in the hospital as it only increased my dosage even more to get my body regulated. My white blood cells were attacking my red blood cells. The one good thing I had working for me during this point in time was my Rheumatologist, Dr. Syed, as she was absolutely phenomenal. I initially had to go to her 3 times a week, then it went to 2 times a week, then it went to 1 time a

LIFE AFTER Lupus "The Healing Process"
Luther T. Collins

week, then it went to biweekly, then it went to monthly, and eventually quarterly over a long period of time. The doctor's office and entire staff were truly amazing as they made an unpleasant situation into a pleasurable visit. They would frequently call and check on me from my initial diagnosis all the way to me relocating from VA to GA in the future.

Mentally I was having a hard time comprehending that I was no longer the physical guy with the S on my chess. In my mind things would go back to normal as soon as I returned home but this was far from the case. I was weak, often tired, frequently restless, and mentally exhausted. My mind was questioning if I would ever return to my old self again.

Even as a man I would often find myself to be very playful and a prankster. I skipped a lot of my childhood growing up due to

LIFE AFTER Lupus "The Healing Process"
Luther T. Collins

unforeseen circumstances, but I never missed out on a shortage of having a good time as a grown man. With that being said, I was no longer the same kid growing up in East Ocean View in Norfolk, VA who would go to the beach daily. The doctors explicitly told me to stay out of the sun, cover up, and adopt sunscreen as my new best friend before being released.

As the head of my household, primary provider, father, husband, general manager, youth counselor, son, ministry leader, motivational speaker, natural born leader, poet, performer, and man of many hats it was not easy being in this position. I would go from Mr. Fix It to Mr. needing to be fixed. At home I was unable to take out trash and do my normal everyday routines because I lacked the strength and energy to do so. I physically had to put my cape in the closet and go into Clark Kent mode.

LIFE AFTER Lupus "The Healing Process"
Luther T. Collins

For anyone who truly knows me they know I'm high energy, over the top, and a little extra all the time. I'm what you would consider to be the life of the party. At this stage of my life, I found my light to be dim and flickering. While I was grateful to be out of the hospital I was in a place and position where I had to learn how to live life again. I was at the mercy of God as I often found myself in a dark space trying to make sense of this.

The medication would neutralize the pain, but it was still a major adjustment. I would do minimal exercise daily trying to slowly regain my strength. It was a process as it was like I had to begin life all over again. The major devastation would come when I would attempt to do things that I was doing prior to being hospitalized and diagnosed. Every time I would fall flat on my face as physically, I could not do it.

LIFE AFTER Lupus "The Healing Process"
Luther T. Collins

When you take manhood from a man, is he still a man? What use could he be and to who? How long will I suffer? Will I ever return to my old self? What will people think when they see me now? What happened to Luther T? How will I provide for my family?

These were all the questions I began to ask myself. Carrying this heavy burden of sickness and disease. Having a wife of 5 years and family to provide for. It was almost as if I was handicapped because of my limitations. I could not walk too far, could not drive initially, could not lift, could not entertain any physical activities at all, and the list goes on.

Not to mention I had these rashes all over my body. My face, my hands, my legs, my arms, my head, my back, etc. all covered in rashes. It was hard to rock a bald head with all these rashes everywhere. I began to wear a lot of hats not just because of the sun but because I got tired of the questions. I would

LIFE AFTER Lupus "The Healing Process"
Luther T. Collins

wear long sleeve shirts and pants even on hot days. This kept me from being exposed as much to the sun, but it also covered what appeared to be my new identity at the time.

These weeks at home were slow days for me. I wanted to give up and give in as discouragement wouldn't leave the room because I kept the door open. Mentally I let my thoughts dictate my destiny and physically I let my appearance determine my destination. Because I was weak, sick, hurting, and challenged I became angry. At the time I'm not sure if it was directed at life or lupus.

The denial was the heaviest for me at home because I was out of the hospital and had too much time to think. In the hospital I was fighting for my life not knowing if I would ever make it out. Whereas at home I was fighting for my worth not knowing if I would return to my old self. I constantly tried to pick up where I left off, but the results were always disappointing. It was almost as if I was in a fixed fight where the odds were stacked against me.

In all of the denial God never took his hands off me. Every time I wanted to give up, give in, or just flat out quit all together He would send a light. I was in a dark place, but I can say without hesitation God carried me through as I was too weak to walk on my own. My physical strength and mental strength were gone at this point. He saw what I couldn't see as only He knew what I didn't know.

Segment 3: The Road to Recovery

As time passed my heart would begin to heal as it had been shattered into many pieces. I would begin going places gradually that would insert life back into me slowly. And eventually I began driving short distances that proved to be very encouraging.

First and foremost, this entire road to the recovery process is not achievable, attainable, or accessible without my Lord and Savior, Jesus Christ. I can honestly say that God is so faithful, and he will do just what he said he will do. If it wasn't for his grace and mercy I don't know where I would be. He saved me, covered me, and kept me even when I didn't deserve it. I should have been dead and gone many times, but God. This testimony is a testament to his goodness. I know that God truly has a purpose and a plan for me. I've messed up so many times. I could write a book about my mistakes alone. Man would not understand and would condemn but God said, "Go and Sin No More!"

Church was a big part of this as my Pastor never stopped believing in me and most importantly believing in God. She had that mustard seed faith from the moment she got the first phone call even to seeing me laid up in the hospital in a helpless state. She prayed with me, she prayed for me, and she never lost hope in the healing process. Apostle Vanessa Thomas, I thank you from the bottom of my heart.

I attended Behind the Veil Ministries at this time. I was an usher, head of the drama ministry, and over the media ministry at the time. I would serve faithfully as she saw things in me, I didn't see in myself. I'll never forget when she got a notion that I was a writer, she said you're going to be over our drama ministry, and I said what drama ministry. She said, "The one you will create" as she always pushed me, prayed for me, and picked me. By the grace of God I took the assignment and ran gracefully by writing, producing, and even recording our stage plays. It was an amazing time in God and very encouraging to myself and the people of God. When my marriage was out of balance, she stood in the gap every day until the season shifted. She had a heart of gold and always had an encouraging word for me. She always wanted to know how me and my family were doing.

She even had me speaking at our youth conference and pushed me to be a better man of God. I'll never forget as my very first speaking engagement title was "You are What You Eat!" This was simply stating you are a product of what you put in you and what you hang around. Going to church during this time lifted my spirits because of the overwhelming love. I wanted to get back to work but she made it known

LIFE AFTER Lupus "The Healing Process"
Luther T. Collins

that it wasn't going to happen as I wasn't strong enough yet. This was truly a hospital for me as I got healed spiritually before the mental and physical healing took place.

I would even find strength in going to my doctors' appointments. Dr. Syed was one in a million and the best doctor ever. She was always patient as I could be very stubborn at times. She was always kind and considerate of my needs and feelings at this time. She never stopped checking on me. I never missed an appointment because she was always ensuring that I made each appointment. In fact, she always made room for extra or unscheduled appointments.

I don't remember much about my encounters with her in the hospital because I was truly in and out. But I do remember she was always constantly checking on me. If she was off as soon as she returned to work, she would come by my room first to get an update and check on my well-being. She was heaven sent and a big part of why I'm here today better than ever.

Even her staff was astonishingly amazing and customer eccentric. I don't remember the lady's name at the front desk, but she was great at what she did. She always reflected light and I'm forever grateful for her consistent generosity, encouragement, and transitional joy. And when I relocated to Georgia, I'll never forget she told me to check out, A Piece of Cake, which is altogether lovely!

It's funny because I never enjoyed doctors' visits until this point in my life. I will never forget Dr. Syed's presence in the hospital or when attending her practice regularly. Her team was amazing and a big part of why I'm better than ever before. When I was feeling good, they would encourage me to continue doing the same thing. When I was doing bad, she would change my

LIFE AFTER Lupus "The Healing Process"
Luther T. Collins

medication accordingly as needed and have frequent check ins. I truly felt valued here and that my life was important. They unknowingly inspired me to live while putting me on the fast track on the road to recovery.

My family was a big part of my bounce back. My wife was truly my rib, my strength, my better half, and my everything. We had our make-up and break-up moments as we were both unfamiliar with what a successful marriage looks like. As a result, we had a brief separation some months prior to this. But you would have never known as our bond was stronger than ever at this time. She never left my side during this process. From rushing to my job, waiting for the store to close, staying by my hospital bed, calling family, calling friends and loved ones, bathing me, clothing me, wiping the tears from my eyes, encouraging me, and most importantly praying for me. I can truly say that's love and my wife will forever be my MVP.

My wife and kids surprised me by decorating the house and hanging banners in wait for my arrival home. It felt good to be home and even more so being showered with more love and more gifts. My wife is sweet when she wants to be but please don't get it twisted as she does have some hoodish tendencies that are very well needed. She made sure that I didn't travel by myself outside of a certain radius. She was present at all doctors' appointments when I was first released. She would frequently shut me down or stop me when I was trying to defy gravity and go back to my old self. Even something as simple as taking out trash she would say don't even try it, you know you're not supposed to be doing that.

My wife even planned a strategic trip for my birthday a little over a month after being released from the hospital, which

LIFE AFTER Lupus "The Healing Process"
Luther T. Collins

would prove to be just what I needed. She paid for us to take a local cruise on a small cruise line ship in Richmond. This was very encouraging as I had been discouraged about my weight gain. I was about 30 pounds heavier at this time due to the prednisone and didn't find too many meals that I didn't like. The medication would cause me to eat more, and I wasn't a big fan of weight gain. My wife never mentioned the weight gain as she would always make sure that I ate. On the cruise we ate, we danced, we laughed, we loved, and most importantly we had fun. I had to take breaks in between dancing as I would find myself getting tired.

While I knew I was not myself I felt good about where I was headed. A month prior to this I could not dance lead alone to be on a cruise ship. By this time my medication had me in a safe space in a safe place. As long as I stayed on track with my medication and doctor visits which were beginning to space out due to my steady improvement. Things were looking up and my 33rd birthday was one that I would never forget. That picture is worth a thousand words. Thank you, Tasha, for injecting life back into me and believing in me when I didn't believe in myself.

My mom was my rock as she stayed by my bedside frequently. She kept my family in the loop of what was going on. She would help with the kids and bring them to the hospital to see me during this time. She stayed by my wife's side and let her know everything would be alright. And most importantly she stayed in my ear letting me know that she loved me and that everything would be alright.

My Aunt Brenda was the closest to me at this point in time. She was the one person I could talk to judgment free. We would frequently talk on the phone and share a laugh or two. Aunt Brenda represented strength to me as she had a much bigger battle of her own. She was currently fighting cancer and going to frequent chemo treatments. She had lost her hair, lost weight, and had many challenges of her own. But it never stopped her from being by my bedside. She always smiled, always loved on me, always kept me laughing, and always encouraged me. She never complained as I will forever miss my dear sweet aunt. She could not die then because she was waiting on me to live. May you forever rest in peace Aunt Brenda.

My Aunt Joyce, My Aunt Dot, My Aunt Vonnie, My Aunt Margaret, My Aunt Kathy, My Aunt Jewel, My Uncle Randy, and so many more. Too many to list them all they were all there to love on me. So many cousins, so many friends, and so much family. They never stopped checking on me during this process.

My wife's family who are my family were truly amazing. My mother-in-law, Pastor Cain never stopped praying. My

LIFE AFTER Lupus "The Healing Process"
Luther T. Collins

brothers and sisters in love William, Tony, Ketara, Shanna, and Shereka were all supportive and instrumental in checking on my well-being. My grandma and late grandpa were the best. They were always seeing about me and so encouraging. My Uncle, Pastor Vincent and Aunt, First Lady Cassandra were praying for me.

My Finish Line family showed up and showed out. From phone calls, test messages, and hospital visits there was no shortage of love. From my fellow coworkers to my employees, to my supervisors. I will never forget the love and support you showed me during this time. I will forever be grateful for you all as this meant the world to me.

All these things played a big part in my road to recovery. The hospital and diagnosis were the beginning or first leg of this life relay. Where the denial would prove to be the stagnation point or the second leg of the relay. And the road to

LIFE AFTER Lupus "The Healing Process"
Luther T. Collins

recovery would prove to be the turning point or the third leg of the relay.

LIFE AFTER Lupus "The Healing Process"
Luther T. Collins

Segment 4: Back to Business

By now things were settling in for me as I was shifting into a new norm. The new norm for me was slow progress but I had to learn slow progress is better than no progress. While I couldn't return to my regular scheduled program just, yet I had officially graduated from the handicapped phase. I could officially do things on my own but with limits.

In knowing my boundaries, I would still occasionally test the limits. I was determined that one day I'd not only be back to normal, but I'd be better than ever. By hanging on to this hope I always had something to look forward to. My determination was the driving force behind beating lupus.

My doctor gave me the go ahead for me to return to work. I was out of work for approximately 6 to 8 weeks range. I had some stipulations in returning to work, but I didn't care as I was happy to return. Finish Line was my lifeline and if not the most, one of the enjoyable jobs that I've ever had in my lifetime. I was great at what I did, I enjoyed coming to work, I had a wide customer base, and I had employees who loved and respected me. Prior to leaving work unexpectedly on FMLA our store was on a sales tear pushing our way from the bottom of the company up the ranks in a short period of time. I was determined to pick up where I left off even if on light duty.

I was the store manager at Chesterfield town center mall and our store was strategically located in between a Foot Locker and Champs. So, either way you came in the mall you had to pass another popular shoe store before getting to us. As the leader I made the determination early that we are not in the shoe sales business but that we would be in the customer relations business. I would often tell my employees during interviews the shoes

LIFE AFTER Lupus "The Healing Process"
Luther T. Collins

sell themselves, what can you sell other than a shoe. If you can only sell shoes, then you can't work for me.

We became the ultimate customer destination based on our ability to build relationships. I personally trained all new hires and taught them how to build relationships as our focal point. I truly believe that if you made a personal connection with the customer not only would they buy from you, but they would tell others. And by doing this, customers would bypass other shoe stores to come to us because we threw away the sales hats. Customers would stop by even if not looking for shoes just to chat or check in and would leave with a bag. Customers would order shoes from us that were readily available on the shelf at other shoe stores all because of our customer engagement experience.

And because of this success I was awarded the rookie manager of the year

LIFE AFTER Lupus "The Healing Process"
Luther T. Collins

for the company, Larry Sablosky Customer Service award, At the Bench Award, and other awards on my 2nd official yearly store manager meeting held in Indianapolis, In yearly. This was after completing my first full year as a store manager as I had just made it back to work a couple of weeks before this meeting was to take place. And after seeing the awards from the first visit I took an empty suitcase to Indy. My confidence was through the roof as I just knew I was coming home with many awards, new shoes, bookbags, shirts, etc.

Not only did I come home with a full suitcase, but Chesterfield Town center was officially put on the map. A year later I would win an all-inclusive trip to Cancun, Mexico for two. It was a 4-day 3-night stay for me and my wife. This was a trip and time I will never forget. All these things kept me so busy that it reshuffled my focus and gave me a renewed purpose and passion for life.

LIFE AFTER Lupus "The Healing Process"
Luther T. Collins

On paper I was a sneakerologist or shoe salesman but in real life I was a Customer Service Strategist, Hope Dealer, Turnaround Specialist, and Change Agent. While customer service is not currently in high demand by many employers, this remains to be one of my greatest attributes even today.

In all this success and attention that I was receiving at my job I never forgot my team. I understood that my team helped me get there and I always made sure to show my appreciation frequently. I made sure they were able to get the new releases (friendly in-store competition, bring snacks from time to time, feed workers when permitted, etc.) I invested in my employees and truly promoted from within. Most employers tell you this (usually not always true) as a selling point, but I believed in and wore it on my sleeve.

At that location alone I promoted at least 5 sales associates to management

LIFE AFTER Lupus "The Healing Process"
Luther T. Collins

and at least one made it to store manager. I did hire 3 managers from the outside, but I never neglected to look inside first. And every manager and most associates that have worked for me have gone on to do some amazing things. I'm honored to say that I've managed a doctor, lawyer, Women's college basketball coach (won championship), Engineer/IT, Business Owners, Mechanics, Store Managers, teachers, etc. just at my first store alone.

At work my customers were my heart outside of my employees. I would have kids coming in just to see me and my team. I would have parents coming by with updates on their family. I remember one couple I really enjoyed talking to as they were so inspiring. Mr. Jerry by far became one of my favorite customers as he treated his wife like a queen and was a true father to his son who was big in the sports arena. When they showed up, we rarely talked about shoes, but it was just a good time. When

LIFE AFTER Lupus "The Healing Process"
Luther T. Collins

you can be at work and have a good time then it's not really work. I was in a place and a space where I could motivate, minister, inspire, uplift, encourage, challenge, push, support, promote, and love on everyone who walked through those doors.

I remember a guy named JJ and his work crew as he had his own business who would come mainly for releases only. Our store wasn't big on releases so he would always come through later to buy whatever was left over after the raffle. I started talking to him and his guys and they started coming more outside of release dates. He was heavy into sports as he was a big time Redskins fan. One of his workers was a big time Tarheels fan who is also one of my favorites. So, we connected on a sports lover level. I even attended a Redskins game with the guys by way of invitation. This helped with our sales big time. I never knew what it was to be a

LIFE AFTER Lupus "The Healing Process"
Luther T. Collins

sneaker head until I got into the business and even became one myself.

I was so busy trying to be the top store out of 700 that I forgot about lupus. It was a great distraction and soon I would return to myself. We had loud music in the store so I would often yell funny chants throughout the store to keep everyone laughing. I used to jump over the benches and the chairs in the store. It was nothing for me to run around the store as if it was a track meet. Eventually in time I would return to that guy who was overly competitive and kept everyone on their toes. We had a salesman of the week and even though I was the general manager I still competed just to stay accountable to the team and often won at times, lol.

My life at home was good during this time as everything had fallen into place. My wife and I had our first child together in 2010 after a failed attempt by way of miscarriage in 2009. In 2014

LIFE AFTER Lupus "The Healing Process"
Luther T. Collins

we would welcome in our second child while preparing for a new destination. My wife was a mortgage specialist at Sun Trust Bank for 14 years and I was heavily thriving at Finish Line in what appeared to be a promising career.

I was still taking medication 3 times a day but by now the dosages had decreased some. I was still making my doctors' appointments as I was only going monthly by this time a year plus later. Lupus was physically present and identifiable but in my mind, it was gone. When I gained my confidence, I started speaking and believing God for my healing.

LIFE AFTER Lupus "The Healing Process"
Luther T. Collins

Segment 5: Testing the Limits

By this time, I was really feeling myself. I was overly competitive, arrogant, unbeatable, unshakeable, religious, invincible, above the law, and unstoppable all in my mind. Work was going really well. I was ready to test the limits and get my stunt devil, Evel Knievel on.

I'm not sure how it came about but I decided I wanted to play semiprofessional football for the Richmond Venom. I wasn't the fastest, but I always thought of myself as having sure hands and was a big hitter. And what better way to prove lupus was just a phase than to play semipro football. I was excited and had one of the baddest helmets, so I thought. I enjoyed the practices as we had some big boys on this team, I mean straight up monsters. Solid 300 lb. plus ready to eat your breakfast, lunch, and dinner all in one sitting.

Now in my day I was a force to be reckoned with. I played wide receiver and defensive end. I was drawn to the contact and loved running through even the biggest bodies. In school at a buck 40 I would go head on with the 200 plus lb. linemen and run through them. I remember in middle school in the 8th grade I earned a spot quickly. By dislocating the shoulder of one of my teammates who started at both running back and middle linebacker. I played tight end and defensive end.

Now I was still managing Finish Line as by this time my store was on fire and running on autopilot. We had one of the strongest sales teams as our numbers easily reflected this. My boss would say make sure you get your 40 hours in. And I would do just that, literally 40 on the nose and not a second extra. I informed my team, and we all had an

LIFE AFTER Lupus "The Healing Process"
Luther T. Collins

understanding so it just worked out where I could play football seamlessly. I'm not sure if I was trying to prove something to myself or to make a personal clap back at lupus.

Right before our first game at practice I got injured. This day I'll never forget as I was running a route, and a linebacker fell on my ankle. This guy was about 250 solid, and I can't till this day tell you if I caught the ball or not. I remember being on the ground yelling in pain, as he was getting up off my ankle. I had a partial tear in my Achilles. I ended up going to physical therapy and let's just say there goes my season. I initially had crutches, and it was a long road to recovery at 33.

I was still the store manager at Finish Line as our success was contagious. We were easily one of the top stores in our district. Our district was making waves in the region and companywide. I never stopped showing up to work or practice

LIFE AFTER Lupus "The Healing Process"
Luther T. Collins

and games even while going through physical therapy for my ankle. It was a long unforgettable healing process. I didn't stay off my ankle long enough for it to heal.

Once my wife finally got through to me to stop chasing this football dream, I let it go. Not initially as you couldn't tell me nothing. I was lupus free in my mind and I was that dude. It was time to move on to something else.

That something else was youth counseling as it was always a passion of mine to work with youth. I met a man by the name of Mr. Banks who was the CEO of Brother's Keeper. I would soon work for him part time as a mentor. He told me to become an official counselor I would need a degree in Psychology or Criminal Justice. So, what did I do, got a degree in Criminal Justice.

I was already in school attending Strayer University initially going after a

LIFE AFTER Lupus "The Healing Process"
Luther T. Collins

bachelor's in business. I then switched my major to Criminal Justice in the process. I was primarily online taking occasional challenging courses on the campus. And I even cashed in at Finish Line as they helped pay for some of my education. I finished with an Associates of Arts in Criminal Justice, only needing 6 classes to complete my bachelor's in business.

So, with semipro football with Richmond Venom in my rear-view mirror I decided I wanted to be a youth counselor. I began mentoring young men at Brother's Keeper's and really enjoyed doing this. I would work on my days off from Finish Line creating my own schedule. Mr. Banks became an example, a mentor, a father-like figure, and an inspiration to me. He coached me up, developed me, and showed me the ropes. I will forever be grateful just for the ride along in his Mercedes, time spent in office, computer training, and overall investment in me.

LIFE AFTER Lupus "The Healing Process"
Luther T. Collins

I had to meet with my clients so many hours a week. I would help them with homework, teach them life skills, help with resumes, take them to the library, take them to eat, take them to the store for necessities, attend school conferences with administrators and teachers, take them to the park, meet with their parents or guardians, etc. some were coming fresh out of facilities. Some had small children. They were all teenagers of different ages and different walks of life.

Although this job was short lived it will forever be the most meaningful and memorable jobs that I have ever had. I resigned in November of 2013 after working for 6 months because we were going into the holidays at Finish Line, and I couldn't mess up my bread and butter. I valued my boss, my job, and my clients that much that I refused to give them less than my all. It was bittersweet and a tough decision but I'm

LIFE AFTER Lupus "The Healing Process"
Luther T. Collins

glad I did it. And at Finish Line I valued what we built in a short period of time and was determined to keep pushing forward at all costs.

Holidays in retail are very demanding as I would easily go from 40 hours to 60 plus hours a week with an even greater demand. The mall hours would change, the shipments would increase, the traffic would increase, and my job would be hectic. To stay on top, I would have to take the necessary steps of hiring and training help for the holidays, open up my availability, be flexible, and prepare for long days and long hours. Black Friday during this time was one of the biggest if not the biggest sales day of the year for us. And with Christmas right behind that we had a lot of store changes, new promotions, and preparations that had to take place.

After a successful holiday season and a strong finish to the fiscal year at Finish Line I was ready to see what was next.

LIFE AFTER Lupus "The Healing Process"
Luther T. Collins

Family life was going well as my wife had a chance to get a little bit of shopping out of her system by redecorating the entire apartment not too long after I returned home from the hospital. We took a cruise for my birthday. I got my Associate of Arts in Criminal Justice as she was finishing up her business degree. I was almost fully recovered from my partial Achilles tear from football. We just welcomed a new addition to our family, a beautiful baby girl! And I had just seemed to have my life back as my lupus was being managed so well that it was in my rear-view mirror.

LIFE AFTER Lupus "The Healing Process"
Luther T. Collins

Segment 6: Moving Forward

By now I was on cruise control letting life happen and enjoying the wins in almost every area of my life. My marriage was like a roller coaster at this point only because we had too many voices in our house. Lupus was present as I did have some challenges along the way. But with the help of my Rheumatologist, I was able to successfully navigate the waters without allowing my ship to sink. I was winning big at work, but I still had a desire for much more.

The most important thing to me at this time was my marriage. I didn't want to lose my wife and what we had built in a short period of time. I thought if I could just make it to the 7 year mark things would smooth out for me. It wasn't bad but it wasn't all good as we were still learning how to be husband and wife without having many real-life positive

LIFE AFTER Lupus "The Healing Process"
Luther T. Collins

examples. At this time, we had a beautiful 3-year-old miracle baby and an adorable newborn. Our problem wasn't love or intimacy as we had no shortage of this, but it was not keeping our marriage issues in house. A simple argument becomes much more when mom, friends, and family are involved as we would learn this the hard way.

Lupus was present but by this stage barely detectable by outsiders. Outside of the visual spots on my head and occasional patches here and there you probably wouldn't even know anything was wrong with me. I was much better than ever and stronger than ever, so I thought. The key ingredients to my success at this point are my monthly doctor's visit and consistency in taking my meds. Not only was I flying under the radar, but I was living my best life, so I thought.

In my spare time I always found time to write as I truly believe this was my gift

LIFE AFTER Lupus "The Healing Process"
Luther T. Collins

from God. I began writing my senior year in high school as it all started with a poem entitled, "Come on Over to My Place!" I never knew this would turn into more than a hobby as it all began as therapy, a stress reliever, and a way to express myself without even saying a word. I would write over 500 poems while serving in the US Navy for a brief stint. I was able to win my wife over with the help of heartfelt poetic words. I never knew this would lead to me writing several books. At the present time I was a published author of 4 books, "Occasional Poetry," "Spoken Word," "The Voice I Never Had," and newly released book "Can I Testify!"

At this time, I was preparing for a book signing at the Barnes and Nobles in Chesterfield Town Center Mall which was the same mall that I currently worked at. It was a dream come true and my first official book signing. They truly treated me like a king as I was full of nervousness and excitement. They

LIFE AFTER Lupus "The Healing Process"
Luther T. Collins

offered me food and drinks and whatever I needed without charge. They preordered a certain number of my books prior to the signing. They also created an amazing table stand for me with my book cover and book signing info present. The book signing was a success as I had a lot of my work customers, coworkers, family, friends, church family, and even onsite supporters. After the signing was complete I had maybe 5 books leftover as the manager offered me a spot on the bookshelf in store for the remaining copies. As these books sell, they would order more as I would find them on the shelf even a year later after relocating for my next big opportunity.

Finish Line was so good that I was highly on everyone's radar. I was so much in sync with my team that we never dropped the ball. We grew stronger after my time away due to lupus. I was determined to not only push our team past the limits but to put each and every one of my employees in a position where they could be successful both inside and outside of the company. At this time, I was looking for my next major obstacle as my goal was to get the store to 2 million as we were just over the 1.7 mark. When I officially took over as a new store manager in September 2012 we were at the 1.3 million mark.

Suddenly, a great idea came to me by way of a store vacancy. I wanted to transfer to Atlanta to take over Cumberland Mall which was a 2.3-million-dollar store at the time. I ran it by my wife, and she was excited about a new start. Next, I reached out to my boss and the rest was history from there. My current team surprised me before leaving with an in-house party with cake and celebrations on my last official day at work. We laughed, we cried, we took pictures, and I wrote words of encouragement and comedy on our blue wall by the back door.

LIFE AFTER Lupus "The Healing Process"
Luther T. Collins

My peers as well as upper management warned prior to taking the store by saying you don't want this store as they are in the bottom 10 percent of the company from a profit margin. That was all the motivation I needed to take some vacation days and travel to Atlanta with my wife and our babies before officially accepting the store. I went into the store as no one knew who I was and I saw what no one else saw, unlimited potential. The store was right in front of the food court when you walked in the mall. The store was packed when I visited the store in July of 2014. Everyone was just hanging out behind the sales counter in the back of the store with very minimal to no customer focus. When I returned to VA, I asked my boss when do I leave. I relocated to GA in August of 2014 to be the official store manager of Cumberland Mall.

The transition proved to be a little tough at first as there were so many

LIFE AFTER Lupus "The Healing Process"
Luther T. Collins

moving pieces. The company paid for our out-of-state relocation, which made things a little easier. My wife and our newborn would not move with us until December of 2014 as we traveled back and forth at least once a month. The job transition was not favorable for her, and I had a full plate. It was me and my 2 girls in GA at the time as I would have to drop off and pick up my 3-year-old from daycare daily.

I was so busy with life that I never even gave lupus a thought. I continued to take my medication and would still see my doctor in VA usually once every 2 months now until I was able to find a rheumatologist in GA. I did not realize how hard it could be to find a great doctor until I moved to GA. While I would never find a replacement for Dr. Syed and her office it only made it easier for a God move.

By this time my life revolved around Finish Line as a new store manager I had something to prove. Nobody liked me walking in as my first order of business was to revamp, restructure, and redirect. I wanted to revamp the team and in doing so a lot of team members dropped off initially. I was so big on customer service and building relationships. It wasn't optional as I started with my managers and went down from there. Next, I wanted to restructure our approach by removing the sales hat. No longer will you say how can I help you, what are you looking for, you want to try on that shoe? But we transitioned to what brings you in today, what you got going on today, how's the weather out there, did you see that game last night?

We went from salespeople with I work by commission stamped on our foreheads to finding common ground through genuine conversation. While this did not happen overnight, and we lost a lot of casualties along the way. We eventually arrived going from the very

LIFE AFTER Lupus "The Healing Process"
Luther T. Collins

bottom of the company to the top 5 out of 700 stores percentage wise. We went from a 2.3-million-dollar store to 3.7 million trending to reach 4 million in less than 2 years.

Our biggest competition began to come from our previous year's numbers as we had one of the biggest percentage gain performances company wide. We became so hot that there was no shortage of acknowledgment, awards, promotions, etc. from upper management and company execs. My right hand who was at the store prior to me arriving would soon be promoted to MIT and then to his own store which his success would be a whole other story. Our store was remodeled twice within a two-year period and our product selection became second to none. We went from not having any new products and minimal releases to getting all the newest hottest products in the company. When our company first got the highly anticipated shoes, Yeezy's we were one of the few stores to receive them company wide.

The team was stronger than it had ever been. We had a plug and play system in place where we kept rising superstars on deck for those managers being promoted or going elsewhere. One of our MIT's left to pursue his dreams of being a successful gospel hip hop artist in NY. We had one of our assistant managers leave as she pursued her teaching career. One of our MIT's left for the military. One of our assistant managers got promoted and went to another store. We lost a lot of great individuals, but we also got an opportunity to promote some great upcoming individuals as well. I was always sad to see someone go but I was more encouraged about them leaving for a bigger, better, and brighter future as this was usually the case.

In 2015 my wife and I were able to go to Cancun, Mexico with all expenses

LIFE AFTER Lupus "The Healing Process"
Luther T. Collins

paid. It was a 4-day, 3-night stay courtesy of Finish Line for being one of the top store performers. We were even tracking heavily for the next years trip to Jamica. Things were looking up, so I thought not knowing that Finish Line's future was in jeopardy. Our CEO stepped down, eventually numerous stores would begin closing, and later the company was bought out.

From a health Standpoint I was doing great but there was just one problem. I decided in 2015 to change my doctors. I was not happy at all with my rheumatologist in GA. The office was more business centered than customer friendly. I spaced out my visits as much as possible because I did not like going. It got to the point where I stopped going altogether unless it was absolutely necessary to get a medication refill. I was taking a low dose prednisone, mycophenolate, and hydroxychloroquine at the time.

LIFE AFTER Lupus "The Healing Process"
Luther T. Collins

In 2015 I would also face a nasty custody battle in VA with my ex-wife that ended in me getting custody after 9 years of vicious court battles. On summer vacation she misused her visitation by disappearing altogether and relocating to another state. This was kidnapping obviously but there was nothing I could do physically. GA told me it was nothing they could do and after 10 years of court and excessive resources I decided that I did all I could do, and my fight was done.

At this point my life was so full that I barely had time to even consider lupus. I was determined in my mind that I was lupus free. I was done with the doctor's office in Cobb County. I didn't like the office, the doctor, or the staff. It wasn't anything wrong with them, but they did not provide the customer service I was accustomed to, not even remotely close. I decided that's it I'm officially done.

LIFE AFTER Lupus "The Healing Process"
Luther T. Collins

I was at a place where it was time to believe God for healing and step out on faith. By this time, I was one of the ministers at our newly found church in GA, where I would lead our daily prayer call weekly. I had faith for the world but often would doubt when it came to myself. It was like I would pray and believe God for others' healing, deliverance, and breakthroughs. The individuals I would pray for would even later testify about their breakthroughs because of God using me as a vessel. But when it came to me, I believed God could do it but wasn't sure if he would do it. I soon decided it was time to change my perception as God is not a respect of a person. If he did for you surely, he would do it for me, I adopted his words as my new motto. After many prophecies and much prayer, I was ready to finally go forth believing God that lupus was no more.

Segment 7: Life After

I have not taken any medication or seen any doctors since 2016. I stepped out on faith believing God for complete and total healing of lupus. I would write scriptures and put them in my shoe as I call this walking on the word. By his stripes I am healed. This is one of the ways I began to walk out the word. I brought up the past prophecies and started saying I'm healed.

The type of lupus that I was diagnosed with directly attacks your skin aggressively. My skin would burn, itch constantly, flare up, become patchy, become flaky, etc. in a disrespectful disrupting kind of way. It would wake me up out of my sleep at night as the pain could be intense and unbearable at times. It would lead to other issues, the same ones that landed me in the hospital in 2013. Prior to this I tried winging myself completely off my

LIFE AFTER Lupus "The Healing Process"
Luther T. Collins

medications all with unfavorable outcomes. The medications were designed to minimize and prevent the lifelong damaging effects lupus can have on your body.

Initially I would not say anything until my wife would eventually notice that I placed all my pill bottles on the fridge and had stopped taking them. My wife was like what are you doing? She would say you know what happened last time when you stopped taking your meds. But after a while she stopped mentioning the meds and started agreeing with me. We were enjoying life and learning how to navigate on one accord with this new beginning in GA. We left everything we knew, everyone we loved, and everything familiar to start over in an unfamiliar place.

This time it was more than me being in denial, but it was a God move. I finally decided to walk in God's word for me! Lupus would never have a stronghold

LIFE AFTER Lupus "The Healing Process"
Luther T. Collins

on my life again. My life was so full that I really didn't have time for lupus. I had a wife and kids to provide for. In 2016 my wife also became pregnant again as we would have new challenges to embrace.

In 2016 we had a lot of material possessions but very limited to no wisdom. My wife became sick early in the pregnancy and they told me either her or my son would not make it. We had lots of debt that we accumulated and were operating off two incomes. Once my wife got sick, we lost most of our material possessions. We had 3 cars repossessed in one week. We look back and laugh now but it wasn't funny at the time.

During this time, I was determined to be there for my wife every step of the way. I practically moved into the hospital as she was admitted at 3 months. I would pack up the babies and we would stay with her. We even

LIFE AFTER Lupus "The Healing Process"
Luther T. Collins

celebrated Christmas at the hospital as I decorated a baby tree and put gifts underneath the tree while they were all sleeping. After we got past the health scare with my wife and son, we would soon lose our apartment.

We would move into the Inn Town Suites as we would again be tested. I was working 3 jobs during this time determined to get my family out of the hotel. My wife had fallen into a state of depression, and I became a robot. I was in survival mode just trying to make it through the storm. We attempted to make the best of every situation we faced together. When it was time to enroll our daughter in school it was so embarrassing as they knew we were in a hotel. The Brookwood School district was very rich, and we were very poor at the time as it was just like we didn't fit in at all.

My baby girl was the light in the dark tunnel that we needed to make it out.

LIFE AFTER Lupus "The Healing Process"
Luther T. Collins

My wife would often complain about being trapped in 4 walls with a newborn while she was still recovering herself. Our baby girl would unknowingly become the shining star in our household. She was always smiling as she joyfully walked through the hotel daily with her doll baby in the scroller as she walked her sister to the bus stop with my wife and son. Her laugh would light up the place in the most challenging moments. The days I got phone calls because the couple directly across the hall was fighting or someone was shooting were so devastating. We even had to celebrate Thanksgiving and Christmas in the hotel.

The one bright spot was our church, The Harvest Tabernacle. When we moved to GA, we would travel to VA just to go to church once a month until we found a new church. While we went to other churches, we didn't find our home until we found Harvest. It was my Apostle, Travis Jennings that really

LIFE AFTER Lupus "The Healing Process"
Luther T. Collins

showed me what a real man looks like. As an integral husband, businessman, Pastor, entrepreneur, Author, Life Coach, and so much more he showed me that life gets better with God. My Pastor, Stephanie Jennings was the example of a powerful praying woman who supports her husband while trailblazing in the kingdom.

The more we began to chase after God the easier our journey got. I've learned over the years that sometimes you must go through stuff for the sake of others. I stopped saying whoa it's me, why me Lord, is this repayment for my past, etc. and I started looking to the hills where my help comes from. I started looking to Jehovah Jireh, my provider who is the author and finisher of my faith. God says he would never put more on me than I can bear so I've learned to celebrate. Because this means he's checked my resume to see if I could take it. God has that much confidence in me that he knew I'd make it through.

LIFE AFTER Lupus "The Healing Process"
Luther T. Collins

We made it through the hotel and moved in with a Pastor from our old church. My wife was uncomfortable in a short period of time so that was short lived. We then moved in with one of the Elders from Harvest. He barely knew us but opened his brand-new house to me and my family. For this Elder Frank I will forever be grateful. From there we relocated to a new city that we would call home. A couple of moves later, God put us in this spacious amazingly beautiful home in both of our names attached. We didn't qualify for the house on paper as it was clearly out of our price range, but God!

I have since released several books and launched my publishing company Legacy Voice Productions LLC. as I will never stop writing or creating. My wife and children have all written books. Some released some in the works to be released. The tests and trials are still present but now I look at each obstacle as an opportunity to testify. It was time to fulfill the promise by writing the book.

God has completely healed me from lupus. I have not taken any medication or had any symptoms since 2016, to God be the glory! If God did it for me surely, he can do it for you. It's time to stop being the victim and walk in your healing. I became so busy in life that I didn't have time to entertain the words sickness, disease, diagnoses, death, lupus, affliction, ailment, broken, and grievous. Instead, I intentionally replaced those words with successful, destiny, driven, determined, life, affirmations, abundance, more than enough, anointed, healed, unstoppable, blessings, and God!

You are more than what you have become. It's time to pick up your bed and walk into your destiny! Sickness and disease may cause a delay, but they can't deny your destiny when God is in it! As Prophet Mark Vereen says, "Victory looks like a defeated situation with a but God in the middle!"

My personal testimony is lupus had to die so Luther T could live! What will your testimony be? Write it down, recite it, wear it, walk in it, and receive it! Always remember God's name is greater than your condition. And as my spiritual father Dr. Travis C. Jennings would say, "Your condition is not your concrete conclusion!"

LIFE AFTER Lupus "The Healing Process"
Luther T. Collins

Segment 8: Letter & Poem

Thank you MCV for there will never be enough words to express my gratitude. With God's grace, you saved my life and gave me a 2nd chance to fulfill, build, and create an inspiring life changing legacy. In this segment I have included a copy of the actually letter and poem that I wrote to VCU prior to being released from the hospital.

Thank you Latasha R. Collins, Gail Collins Calendar, Bonita Cain, Apostle Vanessa C. Thomas, Elder Geraldine James (RIP), Behind the Veil, Jewell Jones, Brenda Ford (RIP), my aunts and uncles, Finish Line 554, and all of my family and friends who prayed, visited, and loved me back to life!

God, thank you first and foremost! I thought it was over but you said, "Not so, I still have work for you on earth!" And I shall fulfill the assignment, Lord!

LIFE AFTER Lupus "The Healing Process"
Luther T. Collins

Friday, March 01, 2013

MCV Critical Care Hospital,

    Thank you so much from the bottom of my heart to all the Blood, Hematology, and Rheumatology Doctors. To all the Nursing Staff, Emergency Staff, Dietitians, Care Takers, Pharmacy Staff, and entire Hospital Staff. It has been nothing less than a blessing from God above to put me in well capable hands of people that nursed me back to health and I truly mean this from the bottom of my heart. I went from being down and out to fully restored and set back to mission and purpose that has been personally assigned to me in this lifetime. From myself, my wife, family, friends your generosity, curiousness, endurance, kindness, gentleness, patience, and determination have made this possible. I know nobody's perfect and everything will not always go my way but everyone did their part in ensuring that I had what I needed daily, I did not go without, and all my needs were met. This is coming only after going to other hospitals in the Richmond area and either being turned away or not receiving the proper diagnosis. There are not enough words to express or enough compliments I can give just to show truly how much being here and being coached back to life has forever made a difference in my life. So thank you all as I wish much continued success throughout the entire MCV hospital staff as well as each and every individual in your own personal lives. And last but not lease know that God loves you and I do too today and forevermore.

                        Sincerely Your Friend Forever,

LIFE AFTER Lupus "The Healing Process"
Luther T. Collins

Luther T. Collins
Thank you MCV from Luther T. Collins

Thank you all, MCV Family for everything that you've done in nursing me back to health

For the first time in a while I can actually say I truly feel like myself

From being weak, lifeless, and dead to the world

Just not having enough light to shine with the love of my life, family, or my two year old baby girl

Which just shows life is unpredictable and may throw you curve balls every now and again

But I have been appointed to be anointed and destined by God to win

Chosen, selected, and handpicked on this earth for one true purpose and one true goal

Don't have time to be sick as with the future these many works of art will surely unfold

Your staff, your care, your kindness, your genuineness, and patience will never be forgotten

I can honestly say I was a pain in the butt patient, yet MCV still managed to spoil me rotten

From the many Doctors huddling day and night, determined to find a way to make things right

LIFE AFTER Lupus "The Healing Process"
Luther T. Collins

To the nurses battling with my chills, temperatures, and many symptoms throughout the night

And let's not forget the changing of the gowns and sheets continuously

When that bell sounds, who else could it be other than me

All the while sharing stories back and forth with the workers and staff

Nothing like a sense of humor in a gloomy condition to keep your patient laughing

Thank you all for making the glorious sunshine water down the heavy rain

I'll never forget this experience as love was evident even in the beginning when I knew nothing but pain

I wish you all the best as I know you will continue on each day spreading the love

And may God continue to keep this place showered with his rich blessings from above

Until we meet again I love you all with the most sincerest appreciation

MCV, this is my salute, my farewell, and my special dedication

By: Luther T. Collins

www.ingramcontent.com/pod-product-compliance
Lightning Source LLC
Chambersburg PA
CBHW051702090426
42736CB00013B/2505